Reading notes

This book contains a selection of different recipes that can be consumed relatively well by most people with neurodermatitis. Even though it is obvious, we would like to point out that this book cannot and should not replace medical advice. The book can only be an aid in obtaining recipe ideas that are suitable for everyday use in the implementation of a diet for atopic dermatitis. Thus, this collection of recipes is essentially just a supplement to professional advice.

In the book, it is assumed that those affected have to struggle with "typical" neurodermatitis symptoms. This means that not everyone reacts the same way to all ingredients. Whereas one person may tolerate a handful of strawberries, another person may experience reddening of the skin after eating them. The recipes are therefore based on the typical intolerances of neurodermatitis sufferers.

Although the advice of a nutritionist or doctor is of course decisive in every case, some "rules of thumb" can nevertheless be established. These are basically aimed at giving those who are not affected a little help in cooking - or to serve as a "reminder" for those who are directly affected.

Most ingredients are available in normal shops. It should be noted that individual ingredients are sometimes not available everywhere. By the way, the appropriate diet for neurodermatitis shares this "problem" with numerous other nutritional approaches. Because of this, emphasis has been placed in the book on reducing the use of "exotic" ingredients to the necessary minimum.

A brief compatibility overview

The following statements are, by their very nature, generalisations. In individual cases or in case of doubt, consult a doctor or nutritionist.

Important: If an ingredient is listed as poorly tolerated, this does not necessarily mean that it should be avoided 100%. For example, a squeeze of lemon juice in a dish may be fine - but 3 tablespoons is really not.

The ingredients on the "poor tolerance" list are used sparingly in the book as far as possible. Another example: Person A has found out that she tolerates tomatoes well and can include them in her diet without hesitation. Person B has only "recently" developed atopic dermatitis and still has to find out exactly where the intolerances are - and in case of doubt, avoids tomatoes for the time being.

Cereals, pasta, potatoes and rice
- Mostly well tolerated: millet, oats, spelt, buckwheat, amaranth, quinoa, rice, spelt noodles (egg-free), potatoes.
- Mostly poor tolerance: wheat, rye, sugared muesli, peanut butter, chocolate spreads, durum wheat pasta, soy products, fast food, ready meals (due to numerous additives).

Snacks, nibbles and sweets
- Mostly well tolerated (in moderation): rice cakes, agave syrup, maple syrup, honey, sugar, dried fruit (unsweetened).
- Mostly poor tolerance: Confectionery and bakery products with additives (practically all industrially manufactured products).

Fruit
- Mostly well tolerated: apples (sweet varieties), blueberries, mango, watermelon, apricot, occasionally also bananas and pears.
- Mostly poor tolerance: redcurrant, kiwi, peach, citrus fruits, gooseberry, sour fruits

Vegetables
- Mostly well tolerated: courgettes, asparagus, cucumber, beetroot, mushrooms, chard, sweetcorn, pumpkin, potatoes, broccoli, cabbage, lettuce.
- Mostly poor tolerance: hot herbs, sprouts, chives, pickled vegetables, aubergine, tinned vegetables, onion, tomato, soya bean, celery, sauerkraut, radish, rhubarb, carrot, garlic, ready-made vinegar-oil-based salad dressings.

Nuts, seeds
- Usually well tolerated: pumpkin seeds, pine nuts, almonds
- Mostly poor tolerance: walnuts, hazelnuts, peanuts

Oils and fats
- Mostly well tolerated: olive oil, margarine (without milk), coconut fat (non-hydrogenated), cold-pressed unrefined vegetable oils.
- Mostly poor tolerance: nut oils, lard, sweet cream butter

Drinks
- Usually well tolerated: apple juice spritzer, rice drinks, green herbal teas (lemon balm, fennel, peppermint, etc.), water.
- Mostly poor tolerance: Lemonades of all kinds, alcohol, coffee, black tea, cocoa, soft drinks, fruit tea, other herbal teas.

Fish products and seafood
- Mostly good tolerance: none
- Mostly poor tolerance: all of them (i.e. each ingredient must be tested for individual tolerance).

Meat, sausages
- Mostly good tolerance: turkey, chicken, beef, lamb
- Mostly poor tolerance: pork, spicy products, sausage products with additives.

Dairy products, cheese, eggs
- Mostly good tolerance (in moderation): milk, cow's/sheep's/goat's cheese, kefir, natural yoghurt.
- Mostly poor tolerance: rice pudding, custard, fruit yoghurt, fruit curd, cocoa drinks, blue cheese, cheddar, camembert, brie, parmesan, chicken eggs.

FAQ

"How do I find out which recipes from the book I can cook without hesitation?"

Usually, the doctor or nutritionist will urge you by omission diet to identify potential intolerances.

In practice, this means (simplified description): completely omit all possibly intolerable foods (see list above and the recommendation of your doctor/nutritionist) for 1-2 weeks. The skin condition should now improve (in the case of a diet-related allergy reaction). You can then deliberately include SINGLE foods from the "forbidden list" (e.g. tomatoes) in your daily diet for 1-2 weeks. If the skin condition does not worsen, you can add the ingredient to your "well tolerated foods" list.

"An acquaintance told me that you can get neurodermatitis under control with cortisone cream. Is that true?"

This book cannot and should not give a conclusive medical assessment. Generally speaking, although there are over-the-counter cortisone ointments on the market, their use without medical consultation is not recommended due to numerous potential side effects. In addition, cortisone is said to aggravate atopic dermatitis when used regularly.

"Are there any ingredients that are particularly likely to cause allergic reactions in atopic dermatitis sufferers?"

Too many hot spices, eggs, fish, strawberries, kiwis and also tomatoes can fuel atopic dermatitis. This means that even if you tolerate tomatoes well, for example, you should only consume them in moderation. The same applies to spices. In general, products with colourings, flavourings and preservatives should also be avoided. In most cases, it is not the actual main ingredient that is the trigger, but an additive.

"What does the typical menu look like on a normal day?"

For example: In the morning, muesli with fruit and yoghurt (tolerable varieties, of course). At lunchtime, a meat meal with steamed vegetables and a potato side dish. In the evening, a good soup or a spelt sandwich with a side salad.

"What can I take as a snack for work or on the go?"

A few apples or rice cakes are always good. Dried fruit (without added sugar) as a snack is also good.

"I need to grab something quick to eat on the way - starving myself is not the answer. What fast food should I indulge in?"

Here it can only be a question of "less bad" and by no means "unhesitatingly good". A chicken leg from the grill or a salad (pay attention to dressing additions) is halfway "ok".

"I have been a chain smoker for years. I have already changed my diet, yet my neurodermatitis is not getting better. What am I doing wrong?"

Neurodermatitis can have nutritional causes or be aggravated by a wrong diet - but this does not have to be its main trigger. Other environmental influences can also be considered - e.g. smoking.

"I have read a guidebook, watched a documentary on TV with tips and now I have this book. With all the advice, should I treat my neurodermatitis myself and change my diet?"

No. A change in diet must always be discussed with a doctor or nutritionist. One of the reasons for this is that this book, for example, can only make general statements that do not necessarily apply to your life situation. Rather, the opposite approach is better: first go to the doctor or nutritionist, then get additional suggestions for the concrete implementation with suitable literature and books like this one.

"I have a question about my neurodermatitis. I have had X for years and have already tried Y - should I now start with Z...?"

Please take these questions to a doctor or appropriately trained nutritionist. No book, no internet forum, no spiritual healer and no "hearsay" can or SHOULD give you concrete advice. The only things that are allowed are general guidelines (such as the list above with the ingredients). Only experts are allowed to give concrete statements for reasons of liability and above all for moral and ethical reasons (keyword: wrong treatment).

"but Karlo62 told me in a forum that..."

The internet, books and TV programmes can certainly provide suggestions and tips. In case of doubt, however, the opinion of your doctor or nutritionist is decisive. After all, they are legally responsible for their diagnosis if, for example, you suffer damage as a result.

"...and Someone else meant that certain supplements can also relieve atopic dermatitis?"

At least as a complementary measure. Your doctor or pharmacist can give you sound advice on which products (or which active substances) are suitable for you.

"In one dish I found an ingredient that is on the "less compatible" list. What applies now?"

First and foremost, the statement of your doctor or nutritionist. Additionally, it is often the "dose that makes the poison." Example: A trace of a hot spice will often not trigger an allergic reaction - a hopelessly fiery, generously spiced meal, on the other hand, might. If in doubt, leave out the ingredient or meal until the tolerance has been tested by means of an omission diet. The compatibility list is also a simplification. Theoretically, one would have to classify the ingredients into many more categories (e.g. very well tolerated, well tolerated, tolerated in moderation, mostly poorly tolerated, no tolerance), but then the clarity and practicability of the table, which is only meant to be an aid, would suffer.

"Are the nutritional values in the recipes calculated per portion or for the entire dish?"

The nutritional values refer to the entire meal. If the recipe is given for 3 portions, the nutritional values refer to the 3 portions combined. The nutritional values are subject to the natural fluctuations of food and are rounded values.

"I don't have neurodermatitis at all, but my regular visitor/relative/partner does. I would like to cook a recipe from this book. Can I be 100% sure that this will then be suitable for the person?"

Only the person concerned can answer this question. If questions are not possible or if you want to avoid them (e.g. because it should be a surprise), the recipes in the book can serve their purpose as a rough guideline. At least with the recipes you avoid the "typical, grossest blunders" regarding the appropriate diet for neurodermatitis. As a layman, you cannot and should not be expected to do more. As a host, you are already far ahead of many other people in this respect.

To illustrate this with an example from another nutrition topic: The low-carb eater will enjoy a schnitzel with a large side salad and lots of vegetables, even if the breadcrumbs are not "ideal". All in all, the dish is still relatively low-carb and does not jeopardize the diet completely. If the visitor complains, however, his manners must be doubted. The situation would be different at a reception with a large portion of spaghetti bolognese. This would definitely not be low-carb compliant.

"If there was one piece of advice that could be given regarding the diet for atopic dermatitis - what would it be?"

Probably this would be the complete renunciation of ready-made products of any kind. The flavourings, colourings and additives contained can quickly turn even supposedly "good" ingredients into an allergy-triggering affair. If you follow this credo, you also automatically avoid many unsuitable eating options outside the home (e.g. fast food).

"I like to drink my after-work beer/glass of red wine in the evening. My doctor thinks that this is not good for my neurodermatitis. Is it enough if I just follow his dietary advice and still stick to my beer/wine?"

Maybe it will get better despite beer and wine - maybe not. In any case, it definitely won't be as good as it COULD be.

"Good, I can do without the regular consumption of alcohol. What about an occasional glass at a family celebration?"

The glass of red wine at Christmas will probably do little harm overall, but no general statement can be made here. It is true that for many people the occasional consumption of alcohol is relatively inconsequential in relation to neurodermatitis - but not for everyone. The only thing that helps here is consultation with a doctor or nutritionist.

"Unfortunately, I like coffee a lot. I'm not really allowed to drink black tea as an alternative. What should I do?"

Energy drinks, cola drinks or even coffee tablets are not recommended as a substitute. Many green teas have a weaker but still stimulating effect like coffee. They are therefore the most acceptable substitute.

Drinks

Drinks, smoothies and co.

Spinach melon cinnamon juice

Preparation time: 15 minutes

Ingredients for 1 serving:

½ honeydew melon
250 g young spinach leaves
1 cinnamon stick (round 1 cm)
A pinch of nutmeg
A few ice cubes

Preparation:

1. Remove the seeds from the melons with a spoon. Remove the skin and roughly dice the flesh.
2. Prepare the spinach ready for cooking.
3. Scrape small, thin strips off the cinnamon stick with a knife.
4. Squeeze the spinach. Set aside a few leaves and stalks for decoration. Juice the rest together with the melon.
5. Pour into a glass with ice cubes.
6. Add a little nutmeg on top. Garnish with cinnamon and decorative spinach. Serve and enjoy.

Nutritional values:

82 kcal | 4 g protein | 0 g fat | 15 g carbohydrates

Homemade vegan pistachio milk

Preparation time: 15 minutes

Ingredients for 4 servings/glasses:

150 g pistachio kernels (shelled and roasted)

500 ml water

1000 ml water

4 dates

1 pinch ground tonka bean

1 pinch of ground green tea (ideally use "matcha tea powder")

1 tbsp white almond paste

Preparation:

1. Soak the pistachios in water (500 ml) for 4-5 hours. Then rinse the pistachios well and pour away the water.
2. Puree the pistachios with fresh water (1 litre) and the dates in a blender.
3. Pour the pistachio milk through a very fine sieve into a saucepan. Add the tonka bean, green tea powder and almond paste. Mix well and heat over a medium flame.
4. Once everything is well warmed through, divide the mixture into four portions and transfer to glasses.
5. Close and leave to cool.
6. Alternatively: Serve warm and enjoy.

Nutritional values:

382 kcal | 8 g protein | 24 g fat | 28 g carbohydrates

Homemade melon cold bowl

Preparation time: 15 minutes

Ingredients for 2 servings:

Half a watermelon (around 700-800 g)
4 sprigs lemon thyme (prepared ready to cook)
200 ml vegetable stock
A pinch of salt
A pinch of pepper
3 spring onions (cut into fine rings)
1 tablespoon apple syrup

Preparation:

1. Cut the watermelon half into wedges. Remove the peel. Remove the seeds and cut into bite-sized pieces.
2. Finely purée the leaves of two thyme leaves together with the melon and vegetable stock. Then add salt and pepper.
3. Fry the spring onion rings in a hot pan without fat.
4. Add the apple syrup. Bring to the boil briefly. Then allow to cool to room temperature.
5. Serve the pureed melon mixture sprinkled with spring onions and finished with the remaining thyme.

Nutritional values:

200 kcal | 4 g protein | 0 g fat | 40 g carbohydrates

Coconut date shake with banana

Preparation time: 10 minutes
Ingredients for 4 servings:
150 ml coconut milk
50 ml water
60 g dried dates
2 tbsp maple syrup
1 pinch cinnamon
1 banana

Preparation:
1. Pit the dates, if not already done.
2. Mix all ingredients well in a blender.
3. Serve immediately or chill in the fridge for half an hour.
4. Enjoy.

Nutritional values:
589 kcal | 1 g protein | 7 g fat | 19 g carbohydrates

St. John's Rosehip Tea Bowl

Preparation time: 10 minutes
Ingredients for 10 servings:
1.5 litres rose hip tea (cooled)
350 ml currant juice
50 g honey
A few fresh red currants (alternatively: use frozen berries)
One lemon (cut into decorative slices)
Optional: A few apple pieces

Preparation:

1. Stir together the tea, redcurrant juice and honey.
2. Add the fresh (or frozen) berries.
3. Pour into a large carafe and serve garnished with lemon slices. Optionally add apple pieces.

Nutritional values:

117 kcal | 0 g protein | 0 g fat | 8 g carbohydrates

Strawberry-apple punch

Preparation time: 15 minutes+ resting time

Ingredients for 4 servings:

800 g strawberries (fresh or alternatively frozen)
Juice of two lemons
700 ml apple juice
1 litre sparkling water
A little lemon balm
1-2 tsp raw cane sugar
Optional: A few ice cubes

Preparation:

1. Cut the strawberries into thin slices.
2. Sprinkle with sugar. Add lemon juice.
3. Pour in half of the apple juice. Add a few lemon balm leaves.
4. Leave to infuse for a good two hours.
5. Add the remaining ingredients or the rest.
6. Serve and enjoy.

Nutritional values:

694 kcal | 2 g protein | 1 g fat | 35 g carbohydrates

Apple cocktail with avocado and banana

Preparation time: 10 minutes

Ingredients for 1 serving:

160 ml apple juice
½ banana
40 g avocado
A few ice cubes

Preparation:

1. Blend ingredients in blender (except ice cubes).
2. Then pour into a glass and garnish with ice cubes.
3. Serve and enjoy.

Nutritional values:

627 kcal | 1 g protein | 6 g fat | 23 g carbohydrates

Beetroot smoothie with avocado and banana

Preparation time: 15 minutes

Ingredients for 2 servings:

1 avocado (only the flesh, roughly mashed)
2 bananas (peeled, roughly mashed)
1 piece ginger (finely chopped)
1 beetroot (finely diced)
400 ml coconut water (refrigerator cold)
1 tablespoon linseed oil
1 tbsp. wheat germ oil

Preparation:

1. Mix the ingredients in a blender.
2. Serve and enjoy.

Nutritional values:

780 kcal | 10 g protein | 50 g fat | 74 g carbohydrates

Almond nut smoothie with fruit and herbs

Preparation time: 15 minutes
Ingredients for 2 servings:
½ bunch parsley
2 tbsp almond paste
2 tbsp. lemon juice
300 ml water
1 tsp linseed oil
1 tsp wheat germ oil

Preparation:
1. Roughly chop the fruit and remove the seeds.
2. Wash the herbs.
3. Mix all ingredients in a blender.
4. Serve and enjoy.

Nutritional values:
667 kcal | 10 g protein | 34 g fat | 78 g carbohydrates

Good Morning Cocoa with Guarana

Preparation time: 10 minutes

Ingredients for 1 serving:

2 tsp cocoa (low fat)
1 tsp guarana
1 pinch cumin
1 pinch nutmeg
1 pinch coriander
150 ml milk (low fat)

Preparation:

1. Warm the milk slightly in a saucepan.
2. Add all the ingredients to the pot. Mix well.
3. Stir vigorously until the cocoa has dissolved.
4. Pour into a glass and enjoy.

Nutritional values:

118 kcal | 8 g protein | 4 g fat | 12 g carbohydrates

Turmeric date shake

Preparation time: 10 minutes

Ingredients for 1 serving:
1 banana
1 tablespoon coconut oil
2 dates
200 ml milk
50 ml cashew milk
1 tsp turmeric
1 pinch black pepper

Preparation:
1. Peel the bananas and mash them coarsely.
2. Blend with remaining ingredients in a blender.
3. Put everything in a glass.
4. Serve and enjoy.

Nutritional values:
300 kcal | 7 g protein | 12 g fat | 40 g carbohydrates

Salads
Tasty ideas for every day

Pear and fennel cress salad

Preparation time: 15 minutes
Ingredients for 2 servings:
2 fennel bulb (prepared ready to cook)
1 pear (quartered and cored)
Juice of one lime
1 bunch watercress (prepared ready to cook and cut into bite-size pieces)
1 tsp sesame oil
1 pinch of salt
1 pinch of pepper

Preparation:
1. Thinly slice the pear and fennel. Place in a bowl.
2. Add the lime juice to the bowl.
3. Add the cress. Drizzle with sesame oil.
4. Salt and pepper.
5. Serve and enjoy.

Nutritional values:
198 kcal | 10 g protein | 4 g fat | 26 g carbohydrates

Olive pasta salad with peas

Preparation time: 30 minutes

Ingredients for 4 servings:

200 g snap beans (beans cut into fine strips)
Water (quantity as required)
A pinch of salt
100 g frozen peas
150 g orechiette pasta ("little ear" pasta), or other short pasta variety
2 yellow courgettes (sliced)
One jar of black olives (sliced, around 30 g)
4 sprigs lemon thyme (ready to cook, coarsely chopped)
5 tbsp white wine vinegar
A pinch of pepper
3 tbsp olive oil

Preparation:

1. Cook the beans in boiling water (with a pinch of salt) for two minutes. Add the peas. Cook for another three minutes.
2. Drain the pea and bean mixture. Rinse briefly in cold water, drain and set aside.
3. In the meantime, prepare the pasta according to the package instructions.
4. Add the courgettes to the pea and bean mixture.
5. Drain the olives and add them together with half of the thyme.
6. Drain the finished pasta, rinse in cold water and add to the vegetables.
7. Mix the vinegar, salt, pepper and remaining thyme in a bowl. Whisk in the olive oil.
8. Add the sauce from step 7 to the vegetable-pasta mixture and leave to rest for 20 minutes.
9. Season the finished salad with salt and pepper if necessary.
10. Serve and enjoy.

Nutritional values:

1080 kcal | 36 g protein | 44 g fat | 12 g carbohydrates

Spinach and avocado salad with cress

Preparation time: 25 minutes
Ingredients for 2 servings:
150 g young spinach leaves (prepared ready to cook)
Juice of half a lemon
1 tbsp elderflower syrup
1 pinch of salt
1 pinch of pepper
1 tablespoon germ oil
1 small avocado
12 nasturtium flowers (optional garnish)

Preparation:

1. Mix the lemon juice with the syrup, salt, oil and pepper to make a sauce. Season to taste if necessary.
2. Peel, halve and pit the avocado. Then cut the flesh into wedges.
3. Mix the avocado pieces with the sauce. Add the spinach. Mix well. Add salt and pepper.
4. Serve on plates garnished with cress flowers.

Nutritional values:
450 kcal | 6 g protein | 40 g fat | 12 g carbohydrates

Watermelon Salad with Mint and Pistachio

Preparation time: 35 minutes

Ingredients for 4 servings:

One watermelon

6 dates

Juice of one lime

2 tbsp agave syrup

40 g pistachio kernels (chopped)

4 stalks mint (ready to cook, finely chopped)

Preparation:

1. Cut the watermelon in half.
2. Cut out balls with a ball cutter.
3. Pit the dates. Cut into pieces.
4. Mix the dates, lime juice and agave syrup.
5. Add to the melon balls.
6. Leave to infuse in the fridge for a good 20 minutes.
7. Sprinkle melon balls with mint and pistachio.
8. Serve and enjoy.

Nutritional values:

900 kcal | 16 g protein | 24 g fat | 154 g carbohydrates

Buckwheat tomato and bean salad

Preparation time: 50 minutes + resting time

Ingredients for 4 servings:

200 g buckwheat
500 ml water
20 Vegetable broth (yeast-free)
500 g green beans (cut into bite-sized pieces)
500 g tomatoes (sliced)
400 g shallots (sliced)
4 tbsp. oil
1 tsp chives
1 tsp basil
1 tsp savory

Optional: Additional spices of your choice

Preparation:

1. Boil the buckwheat with the water and stock in a pot.
2. Cover and leave to rest overnight.
3. The next day, boil again in the same pot with the brew-refined water.
4. Add the beans to the pot. Cook for 30 minutes. Add the savory and basil as well.
5. Pour off the liquid from the pot.
6. Pour the contents of the pot into a bowl. Add the tomatoes and shallots.
7. Season with the remaining spices/herbs and oil.
8. Leave to infuse for a good hour.
9. Serve and enjoy.

Nutritional values:

820 kcal | 13 g protein | 10 g fat | 55 g carbohydrates

Carrot and sultana salad

Preparation time: 45 minutes
Ingredients for 2 servings:
30 g grated coconut
50 g sultanas
250 ml water
250 g carrots (grated)
1 tbsp. oil

Preparation:
1. Mix the sultanas and coconut in a bowl.
2. Bring the water to the boil in a saucepan.
3. Then add to the bowl.
4. Cover and leave to infuse for 30 minutes.
5. Add the carrots.
6. Add the oil and mix well.
7. Serve and enjoy.

Nutritional values:
1600 kcal | 4 g protein | 20 g fat | 50 g carbohydrates

Chicory salad with apples and oranges

Preparation time: 15 minutes + resting time

Ingredients for 2 servings:
150 g chicory (chopped)
2 apples (diced)
2 oranges (cut into small pieces, without peel)
Juice of two lemons
1 tbsp. oil
Optional: A little stevia

Preparation:
1. Mix the oil and lemon juice.
2. Add the chicory leaves and the centre pieces.
3. Add the apple and orange.
4. Mix well.
5. Leave to infuse for a good hour.
6. Sweeten with stevia if necessary.
7. Serve and enjoy.

Nutritional values:
1260 kcal | 8 g protein | 8 g fat | 46 g carbohydrates

Lentil and pumpkin salad from the oven

Preparation time: 50 minutes
Ingredients for 1 serving:
1 handful radicchio (in strips)
1 handful rocket
1 handful lamb's lettuce
5 radishes (sliced)
A handful of radish sprouts (prepared ready to cook)
1 handful of grapes (red, halved, without seeds)
½ avocado (diced)
1 tablespoon lemon juice
1 pinch of salt
1 pinch of pepper
40 g cardinal lentils
250 g pumpkin (variety: Hokkaido, cut into wedges)
1 tablespoon parsley
Dressing:
3/2 tsp grainy mustard
3 tsp maple syrup
3 tsp apple cider vinegar
Water (quantity as required)
A little salt
Some pepper

Preparation:

1. Place the radicchio, rocket, lamb's lettuce, radish and radish sprouts in a bowl. Add the avocado, lemon juice, salt and pepper to the bowl. Mix well.
2. Prepare the lentils according to the instructions on the packet. Then leave to cool.
3. In the meantime, preheat the oven to 200 degrees.
4. Cook the pumpkin on a baking tray lined with baking paper for 30 minutes until soft.
5. Meanwhile, mix the dressing ingredients and add water if necessary if it becomes too thick.
6. Add the lentils and most of the dressing to the bowl. Mix well.
7. Arrange the cooked pumpkin on top. Pour over the rest of the dressing.
8. Serve and enjoy.

Nutritional values:

445 kcal | 17 g protein | 16 g fat | 56 g carbohydrates

Desserts, sweets and co.

Dessert and neurodermatitis do not have to be mutually exclusive

Simple apple compote

Preparation time: 25 minutes

Ingredients for 4 servings:

800 g apples (tart variety, corresponds to approx. 4 apples)
50 g coconut blossom sugar
1 cinnamon stick
3 grains allspice
200 ml apple juice

Preparation:

1. Peel and core the apple.
2. Then dice the apple.
3. In a saucepan over medium heat, caramelise the coconut blossom sugar (it should already be light brown).
4. Add the allspice and cinnamon.
5. Add the apple juice. Bring to the boil, stirring constantly, until the caramelised coconut blossom sugar has completely dissolved.
6. Add the apple pieces.
7. Steam on a low flame for 12 minutes. Stir occasionally.
8. Pour into a bowl and leave to cool.

Nutritional values:

800 kcal | 4 g protein | 0 g fat | 200 g carbohydrates

Indian style crêpes

Preparation time: 90 minutes + preparation time
Ingredients for 4 servings:
180 g basmati rice
130 g Indian lentils (split)
Water (quantity as required)
½ tsp cane sugar
A little salt
750 g potatoes (mainly waxy)
2 bunches spring onions (chopped)
4 tbsp. oil
1 tbsp brown mustard seeds
1 tsp coriander seeds
1 tsp ground cumin
1 tsp ground ginger
1 tsp ground turmeric
300 ml coconut milk (9% fat)
Some pepper
12 stalks coriander
150 g mango chutney

Preparation:

1. Soak the rice and lentils each in a bowl of water overnight.
2. Drain the water from the rice and lentils.
3. Puree the rice and lentils separately. If necessary, add a little water to make it nice and mushy.
4. Only then mix the purees with sugar and 2 tsp salt.
5. Cover with cling film. Leave to ferment overnight at room temperature.
6. Boil the potatoes with their skins in the pot and water to cover for about 20 minutes.
7. Drain briefly and leave to cool. Peel, coarsely dice.
8. Fry the mustard seeds in a pan with 3 tbsp oil over a high flame. Stop as soon as it starts to "crackle", which should take about 10-30 seconds (once the oil is hot).
9. Add the coriander and spring onions. Sauté on a low flame for four minutes, stirring constantly.
10. Add the cumin, ginger and turmeric, potato and coconut milk. Season with salt and pepper. Cover and cook over a medium heat for ten minutes.
11. Mash the potatoes a little. Keep the whole thing warm.
12. Stir the ready dough briefly. The consistency should be quite thin; if not, add more water if necessary.
13. Brush the pan with the remaining oil.
14. Add about 4-5 tbsp of batter and spread on the bottom of the pan. Fry for one minute per side. Then transfer to plates immediately. Repeat with the rest of the batter.
15. Place the crêpes on a plate and cover with a damp cloth and place in the oven at 80 degrees (to keep warm).
16. Arrange the potato filling, coriander and chutney together in bowls.
17. Fill one crêpe with the potato-coriander-chutney mixture.
18. Sprinkle with coriander, fold and serve.

Nutritional values:

2360 kcal | 56 g protein | 68 g fat | 368 g carbohydrates

Quinoa waffles with millet

Preparation time: 40 minutes
Ingredients for 4 servings:
200 g quinoa (cooked)
400 g millet (ground)
Water (quantity as required)
1 tbsp oil (rapeseed or safflower oil recommended)
Topping for the waffles (e.g. a little apple sauce)

Preparation:

1. Cook the quinoa according to the package instructions.
2. Mix millet with quinoa and water to form a dough.
3. Prepare in the waffle iron on the high setting according to the instructions for use of the appliance.
4. Serve homemade waffles and enjoy - optionally top with apple sauce.

Nutritional values:

2310 kcal | 17 g protein | 9 g fat | 95 g carbohydrates

Quinoa-based muffins

Preparation time: 50 minutes
Ingredients for 6 servings:
250 g quinoa flour
1 tsp salt
1 packet cream of tartar baking powder
5 g guar gum
2 tbsp oil of choice
400 ml sparkling water
clarified butter (quantity as required)

Preparation:

1. Preheat the oven to 200 degrees.
2. Grease the muffin tin with clarified butter.
3. Mix the quinoa flour, salt, cream of tartar baking powder and guar gum in a bowl until well combined.
4. Add the oil and the bubbly. Work into a smooth dough.
5. Fill the muffin tin with batter.
6. Bake in the oven for just under half an hour.
7. Then leave to cool for 15 minutes.
8. Serve and enjoy.

Nutritional values:

740 kcal | 5 g protein | 5 g fat | 177 g carbohydrates

Roasted figs with honey

Preparation time: 20 minutes

Ingredients for 4 servings:

250 g figs (quartered)
1 tablespoon honey
1 tablespoon water
1 tablespoon lemon juice
½ tbsp. clarified butter
1 tsp rosemary

Preparation:

1. Mix the water, lemon juice and honey.
2. Heat the clarified butter in a pan.
3. Add the rosemary and figs.
4. Fry for two minutes.
5. Mix in the honey mixture.
6. Continue to stir-fry until everything has caramelised slightly and become thick.
7. Serve while still warm and enjoy.

Nutritional values:

1320 kcal | 3 g protein | 32 g fat | 44 g carbohydrates

Almond-hazelnut chocolate

Preparation time: 15 minutes + resting time
Ingredients for 1 bar:
25 g hazelnuts (alternative: almonds)
15 g erythritol (ground)
40 g coconut oil
15 g hazelnut flour
A little vanilla powder
1 pinch cinnamon
1 pinch cocoa

Preparation:

1. In a pan, caramelise the hazelnuts with the sweetener erythritol.
2. Mix the remaining ingredients and add the pan contents.
3. Stir well so that the mixture becomes liquid and can be poured into a mould.
4. Transfer to the mould and leave to rest in the fridge overnight.
5. Serve the next day (or as desired) and enjoy.

Nutritional values:

618 kcal | 12 g protein | 66 g fat | 18 g carbohydrates

Chickpea snack with turmeric

Preparation time: 30 minutes

Ingredients for 4 servings:

1 can chickpeas
1 tbsp rapeseed oil
1 tsp turmeric
1 tsp caraway
1 tsp smoked salt

Preparation:

1. Sieve the chickpeas and rinse with water. Pat dry.
2. In a bowl, mix the chickpeas with the remaining ingredients.
3. Roast in a pan over medium heat for twenty minutes. Stir occasionally.
4. Ready when the chickpeas are brown and crispy.
5. Leave to cool a little. Serve and enjoy.

Nutritional values:

420 kcal | 20 g protein | 16 g fat | 48 g carbohydrates

Crispy muesli with seeds and amaranth

Preparation time: 40 minutes

Ingredients for 5 servings:

1 banana
3 tbsp. coconut oil
1 tablespoon honey
100 g oat flakes
3 tbsp. linseed
3 tbsp pumpkin seeds
3 tbsp sunflower seeds
3 tbsp puffed amaranth
30 g almonds (chopped)
1 tsp cinnamon

Preparation:

1. Preheat the oven to 150 degrees.
2. Peel the banana. Mash with coconut oil and honey in a bowl.
3. Add the remaining ingredients. Mix well.
4. Place on a baking tray lined with baking paper.
5. Bake for 30 minutes - stirring every ten minutes.
6. Ready when the muesli has turned golden brown.
7. Leave to cool and serve.

Nutritional values:

1340 kcal | 50 g protein | 375 g fat | 120 g carbohydrates

Baked apple with cinnamon and jam

Preparation time: 10 minutes

Ingredients for 4 servings:

4 apples (cored with an apple corer)
1 tsp cinnamon
2 tablespoons jam
2 tbsp almonds (chopped)

Preparation:

1. Preheat the oven to 180 degrees.
2. Mix the cinnamon, jam and almonds in a bowl.
3. Pour the mixture into the apples.
4. Place the apples in a baking dish.
5. Bake in the oven for a good twenty minutes.
6. Serve and enjoy.

Nutritional values:

600 kcal | 8 g protein | 12 g fat | 111 g carbohydrates

Good things from the pan
From classics to unusual ideas

Date courgette ginger pan-fried vegetables

Preparation time: 70 minutes

Ingredients for 4 servings:

1 kg courgettes (cut into thick slices)
2 bunches spring onions (cut into 2 cm pieces)
1 piece of ginger (finely grated, alternatively: use powder)
50 g dates (pitted, cut into fine strips)
3 tbsp rapeseed oil
A pinch of salt
A pinch of pepper
Juice of one lemon
6 coriander stems (prepared ready to cook)

Preparation:

1. Mix the dates with the ginger.
2. Fry the courgettes in batches in a Teflon pan in 1 tbsp rapeseed oil for five minutes each. Season with salt and pepper. Then mix with the date-ginger mixture.
3. Heat the remaining rapeseed oil in the pan. Fry the spring onions in it for a good five minutes. Season with salt and pepper, then add to the ingredients from steps 1 and 2.
4. Drizzle lemon juice over everything. Mix well. Cover and leave to marinate for 30 minutes.
5. Add the coriander. Salt and pepper again if necessary.
6. Serve and enjoy.

Nutritional values:

722 kcal | 16 g protein | 31 g fat | 76 g carbohydrates

Coconut aubergine curry with rice

Preparation time: 50 minutes
Ingredients for 4 servings:
4 tsp coriander seeds & 1 tsp cumin seeds
2 shallots (finely diced)
1 piece of ginger (finely grated or diced)
3 cloves of garlic (crushed)
2 green chillies (roughly chopped)
2 tsp rapeseed oil
½ tsp turmeric
1 tbsp tamarind paste
400 ml coconut milk (9% fat)
A little salt & some pepper
200 g basmati rice
1 large aubergine (cut into thick slices)
4 stalks Thai basil (ready to cook, coarsely chopped)
Juice of one lime

Preparation:

1. Preheat oven to grill function. Roast the seeds in a pan without fat. Then set aside to cool. Now pound coarsely in a mortar.
2. Heat 1 tsp rapeseed oil in a Teflon pan. Sauté the shallots and garlic for a good three minutes. Add the chilli and ginger and sauté briefly.
3. Add the coriander, cumin, tamarind paste, coconut milk and turmeric. Bring to the boil, then reduce the resulting sauce over medium heat. Season with salt and pepper.
4. In the meantime, prepare the basmati rice according to the package instructions.
5. Fry the aubergine in batches in a grill pan until golden brown and lightly salt.
6. Grease the casserole dish with some of the remaining oil. Place the aubergines in the baking dish with the fried side down and spread well. Pour over the sauce.
7. Bake for 8-10 minutes in the oven with the grill function.
8. Serve the finished dish from the oven with rice and the remaining ingredients.

Nutritional values:
1208 kcal | 20 g protein | 40 g fat | 180 g carbohydrates

Potatoes with curry leaves and caraway seeds

Preparation time: 75 minutes

Ingredients for 4 servings:

1 kg potatoes (mainly waxy)
Water for the potatoes
2 tsp mild curry powder
1 tsp chilli powder
1 tsp turmeric
1 pinch of salt
3 bunches spring onions (cut into 1 cm wide pieces)
3 tbsp. oil
15 curry leaves
1 cinnamon stick
1 tsp brown mustard seeds
1 tsp cumin
Juice of half a lemon
A pinch of pepper

Preparation:

1. Wash the potatoes and boil them with their skins in a pot with water and a little salt.
2. Leave to cool. Then cut into wedges and remove the peel.
3. Mix with curry powder, chilli powder, turmeric and salt.
4. Heat the oil in a pan and fry the potatoes over a high heat for 3-4 minutes, turning frequently.
5. Turn down the heat. Add the curry leaves, mustard seeds, cinnamon and cumin. Fry for one minute.
6. Stir in the spring onion - fry for another five minutes. Refine with pepper and lemon juice.
7. Serve and enjoy.

Nutritional values:

1000 kcal | 16 g protein | 28 g fat | 152 g carbohydrates

Pasta with beans, pesto and pine nuts

Preparation time: 30 minutes
Ingredients for 2 servings:
180 g green beans (cut into bite-sized pieces)
150 g tagliatelle (preferably wholemeal) or other long cooking pasta
Water for the pasta
A pinch of salt
20 g parmesan (grated)
1 tablespoon olive oil
1 tbsp pine nuts
2 tbsp pesto
A little pepper

Preparation:

1. Prepare the pasta according to the package instructions.
2. Ten minutes before the end of the pasta cooking time, add the beans and cook.
3. Toast the pine nuts with a little oil in a pan over a low heat, stirring constantly, until light brown.
4. Drain the pasta and bean mixture. Set aside 1 tbsp of the cooking water.
5. Briefly rinse the pasta and bean mixture with hot water and drain in a bowl.
6. Add the pasta and bean mixture and the one tablespoon of cooking water to the seeds in the pan. Mix with the pesto and Parmesan. Season with salt and pepper.
7. Serve and enjoy.

Nutritional values:
910 kcal | 40 g protein | 38 g fat | 100 g carbohydrates

Indian fish curry

Preparation time: 60 minutes
Ingredients for 4 servings:
200 g long grain rice
Water for the rice
Juice of one lime
1 piece ginger
½ tsp black mustard seeds
1 tbsp unpeeled sesame seeds
1 tsp coriander seeds
600 g catfish (or another light-coloured fish fillet)
1 white onion (diced)
4 tomatoes (diced)
2 tbsp. sesame oil
1 tbsp red curry paste
½ tsp turmeric
300 ml coconut milk
A little salt
6 stalks coriander (ready to cook, coarsely chopped)

Preparation:

1. Prepare the rice according to the package instructions.
2. Mix the lime juice, ginger, mustard seeds and the seeds.
3. Prepare the fish ready to cook and cut into large pieces.
4. Pour the marinade from step 2 over the fish. Leave to marinate for 20 minutes.
5. Heat the sesame oil in a pan. Remove the fish fillets from the marinade and briefly pat dry. Then salt and fry in the pan over a medium heat for a good five minutes. Turn once.
6. Remove the fish from the pan and set aside.
7. Fry the onions briefly in the pan. Stir in curry paste and turmeric.
8. Add the marinade and coconut milk. Bring everything to the boil.
9. Add the tomatoes. Now add the fish again. Allow everything to warm through for 2-3 minutes.
10. Season with salt if necessary.
11. Pour half of the coriander over the pan contents.
12. Arrange on plates with the rice and serve. Sprinkle the rice with the remaining coriander.

Nutritional values:

2194 kcal | 128 g protein | 108 g fat | 176 g carbohydrates

Scampi mushroom tomato skewers

Preparation time: 45 minutes

Ingredients for 1 serving:

150 g scampi

1 tablespoon lemon juice

1 pinch sea salt

1 pinch of pepper

1 tsp oregano

2 spring onions (cut into bite-sized pieces)

100 g mushrooms

1 large tomatoes

1-2 tbsp. coconut oil

4 skewers

Preparation:

1. Prepare the scampi ready to cook (rinse, pat dry) and sprinkle with lemon juice.
2. Salt, pepper and sprinkle with oregano. Cover and chill in the refrigerator for half an hour to set.
3. Alternate onion pieces, tomatoes and scampi on skewers. Season with salt and pepper if necessary.
4. Heat the coconut oil in a pan.
5. Fry the skewers on both sides for about 8-10 minutes.
6. Serve and enjoy.

Nutritional values:

1100 kcal | 30 g protein | 13 g fat | 6 g carbohydrates

Wild boar medallions with quinces and mushrooms

Preparation time: 40 minutes
Ingredients for 2 servings:
40 g quinces (peeled, in strips)
Water (quantity as required)
2 bay leaves
A few peppercorns
A few juniper berries
150 g porcini mushrooms
300 g wild boar saddle
1 large onion (diced)
Salt (quantity as required)
Pepper (quantity as required)
1 tbsp. oil
clarified butter (if necessary)

Preparation:
1. Cover the quinces with water in a saucepan. Salt and add two bay leaves, peppercorns and juniper berries.
2. Cook for a good twenty minutes until soft.
3. Drain with a sieve. Put the resulting broth aside in the pot.
4. Halve the mushrooms.
5. Cut the meat into metal ions. Salt and pepper.
6. Fry the meat with oil in a pan for three minutes on both sides.
7. Then set aside and keep warm (e.g. in the oven at 50 degrees).
8. Add the onion and mushrooms to the pan. Salt and season if necessary. Sauté briefly and deglaze with the stock. Then let it boil down a little. If necessary, add clarified butter.
9. Serve the meat with the sauce poured over it.

Nutritional values:
1630 kcal | 64 g protein | 0 g fat | 7 g carbohydrates

Sliced meat with mushrooms and potatoes

Preparation time: 40 minutes
Ingredients for 4 servings:
800 g potatoes
Water for the potatoes
2 carrots (in strips)
500 g pork fillet (cut into strips)
250 g mushrooms (sliced)
1 spring onion (cut into rings)
2 onions (finely chopped)
3 tbsp. oil
130 ml vegetable stock (yeast-free)
A little sea salt
Some pepper
A little parsley (finely chopped) to garnish

Preparation:
1. Cook the potatoes in a pot of salted water.
2. Sauté the onions in a pan with oil.
3. Pepper the meat. Then add to the pan. Sear well. Then set aside and keep warm (e.g. in the oven at 50 degrees).
4. Now fry the mushrooms and spring onion well. Deglaze with stock.
5. Add the meat. Season to taste and simmer for a few minutes.
6. Season if necessary and serve sprinkled with parsley and boiled potatoes.

Nutritional values:
6000 kcal | 120 g protein | 37 g fat | 142 g carbohydrates

Rice-vegetable pan with chicken

Preparation time: x minutes
Ingredients for 2 servings:
130 g wild rice
1 pepper (cut into strips)
1 courgette (sliced)
1 tbsp. coconut oil
250 g chicken breast fillet (cut into mouth-sized pieces)
1 tsp turmeric
1 pinch of salt
1 pinch of pepper

Preparation:
1. Prepare the rice according to the package instructions.
2. Brown the meat in a pan with the fat. Then set aside.
3. Now cook the vegetables in the pan for 4-5 minutes.
4. Add the finished rice, the meat and the remaining ingredients to the pan. Season again if necessary. Mix well and leave to stand for a minute.
5. Serve and enjoy.

Nutritional values:
920 kcal | 76 g protein | 26 g fat | 102 g carbohydrates

Jerusalem artichoke chicken breast fillet with chives

Preparation time: 25 minutes
Ingredients for 2 servings:
400 g Jerusalem artichoke (peeled, sliced)
3 tbsp. oil (divided into 1x2 and 1x1)
300 g chicken breast fillet (divided into two portions)
A pinch of salt
A pinch of pepper
1 tsp paprika powder (sweet)
A handful of chives (cut into fine strips)

Preparation:

1. Fry the Jerusalem artichokes with oil (2 tbsp.) in a pan for one minute until hot, then continue to cook over medium heat. Turn and fry until golden brown and soft inside.
2. Fry the meat in a second pan with the remaining oil. Season with salt and pepper.
3. Salt and pepper the Jerusalem artichokes and season with paprika powder. Place on plates with the meat and sprinkle with chives.
4. Serve and enjoy.

Nutritional values:

746 kcal | 79 g protein | 33 g fat | 98 g carbohydrates

Grilled melon with pesto

Preparation time: 35 minutes

Ingredients for 4 servings:

1 watermelon (seeded, rind removed, flesh cut into eight slices)
6 macadamia nuts (finely chopped)
2 tablespoons flaked almonds
2 bunches lemon balm (prepared ready to cook, coarsely chopped)
Juice of half a lime
8 tbsp maple syrup

Preparation:

1. Briefly toast the flaked almonds with the nuts in a Teflon pan without fat. Then leave to cool.
2. Blend the ingredients from step 1 together with the lemon balm well with a hand blender.
3. Add the lime juice and maple syrup. Mix well.
4. Briefly grill the melon slices on both sides in a grill pan.
5. Serve the watermelon pieces with the pesto and enjoy.

Nutritional values:

680 kcal | 8 g protein | 24 g fat | 96 g carbohydrates

Dishes from the oven
For cosy and warm kitchen experiences

Oven jacket potatoes with thyme

Preparation time: 40 minutes

Ingredients for 2 servings:

500 g potatoes, halved (small, young ones if possible)

3/2 tbsp rapeseed oil

A pinch of salt

A pinch of pepper

5 thyme sprigs (prepared recdy to cook - alternatively: use powder)

Preparation:

1. Preheat the oven to 180 degrees.
2. Mix the oil with salt and pepper in a bowl. Cut the thyme into pieces a finger wide.
3. Coat the cut side of the potato halves with the oil-salt-pepper mixture.
4. Place cut side down on a baking tray lined with baking paper.
5. Bake for a good half hour.
6. Serve and enjoy.

Nutritional values:

418 kcal | 8 g protein | 14 g fat | 60 g carbohydrates

Sweet potatoes with spinach garnish and tahini

Preparation time: 35 minutes

Ingredients for 4 servings:

4 large sweet potatoes
Water for the potatoes
600 g young spinach
1 pinch nutmeg
Parmesan (grated, quantity as required)
2 tbsp balsamic vinegar & 4 tbsp olive oil
1 lime
1 tbsp maple syrup
2 tbsp tahini
1 tablespoon sesame oil
Pepper as required & salt as required
1 dash soy sauce

Preparation:

1. Preheat the oven on the grill function.
2. Pre-cook the potatoes with the skin and a little water for 20 minutes until they are almost cooked. Then leave to cool.
3. In the meantime, prepare the spinach ready to cook. Heat a large saucepan and cook the spinach (still wet) in it, covered, for a short time (1-3 minutes). Then drain and leave to drain. Add salt, pepper and nutmeg.
4. Mix the vinegar and oil with pepper and salt to make a dressing.
5. Grate the zest of the lime thinly and squeeze out the juice.
6. Mix the zest and juice with maple syrup, tahini, sesame oil and soy sauce. Salt and season if necessary.
7. Place the potatoes, which are now to be halved lengthwise, on a baking tray lined with baking paper with the cut half facing upwards.
8. Drizzle with the spice mixture.
9. Cook for a good five minutes with the grill function until the potatoes are brown.
10. Mix the dressing with the spinach. Add the Parmesan and serve with the baked sweet potatoes.

Nutritional values:

2280 kcal | 54 g protein | 104 g fat | 264 g carbohydrates

Plaice fillet with asparagus

Preparation time: 45 minutes

Ingredients for 4 servings:

500 g green asparagus
Juice of one lemon
1 bunch dill (ready to cook, finely chopped)
4 plaice fillets
A little salt
A pinch of pepper
2-3 tbsp. butter
150 g crème fraiche
1 tbsp. milk (3.5%)
4 tbsp vegetable stock

Preparation:

1. Preheat the oven to 180 degrees.
2. Wash the asparagus, peel the lower third and cut off the woody pieces.
3. Salt and pepper the fillets.
4. Cut a baking paper into four rectangles. Spread with butter (soft!). Leave a margin all around.
5. Place one fillet in the centre of each. Sprinkle with lemon juice and asparagus. Season with salt and pepper.
6. Fold up the baking paper. Put a tablespoon of vegetable broth in each.
7. Place the baking paper on a baking tray in the oven for around 25 minutes.
8. In the meantime, stir milk and crème fraiche until smooth. Salt, pepper and refine with dill.
9. Then pour the sauce over the finished fillets in the parcels of baking paper.
10. Serve and enjoy.

Nutritional values:

1480 kcal | 84 g protein | 112 g fat | 28 g carbohydrates

Baking beetroots with sauce

Preparation time: 35 minutes

Ingredients for 4 servings:

500 g beetroot (cooked, peeled)
2 tbsp olive oil
1 apple (sour variety), sliced, without peel
1 piece ginger (finely grated)
1 tablespoon sugar
150 ml vegetable stock
A little salt
Some ground cinnamon
2 stalks flat-leaf parsley (ready to cook, coarsely chopped)
1 tsp fleur de sel

Preparation:

1. Cut the beetroot into slices. Then mix with the olive oil.
2. Preheat the oven to 200 degrees. Line a baking tray with baking paper and place the beetroot on it.
3. Bake for 20 minutes, turning once. Ready when the edges are slightly crispy.
4. Caramelise the sugar in a saucepan. Add the stock, apple and half of the ginger. Bring to the boil briefly, then cover and simmer on a low heat for ten minutes.
5. Puree the sauce in the pot. Then bring to the boil again. Add the remaining ginger, cinnamon and salt.
6. Arrange the beetroots on plates. Pour the sauce over it. Serve garnished with fleur de sel and parsley.

Nutritional values:

568 kcal | 8 g protein | 20 g fat | 84 g carbohydrates

Sesame Oven Fries

Preparation time: 50 minutes

Ingredients for 2 servings:

500 g waxy potatoes (stalked)
2 tbsp olive oil
1 tsp turmeric
2 tsp unhulled sesame seeds
A little coarse sea salt

Preparation:

1. Mix the potatoes with the oil and turmeric.
2. Preheat the oven to 180 degrees.
3. Place the potato sticks on a baking tray lined with baking paper.
4. Bake for 3 minutes, turning twice.
5. Roast the sesame seeds in a pan without fat.
6. Coarsely grind the sesame seeds with a mortar and sea salt.
7. Drizzle the finished potatoes with the sesame salt and enjoy.

Nutritional values:

488 kcal | 8 g protein | 24 g fat | 54 g carbohydrates

Mushrooms from the oven

Preparation time: 35 minutes
Ingredients for 1 serving:
250 g mushrooms
100 g onions (sliced)
1 tablespoon lemon juice
A little thyme
A pinch of sea salt
A pinch of pepper
1 tbsp. oil

Preparation:
1. Preheat the oven to 230 degrees.
2. Prepare the mushrooms ready for cooking - ergo clean and wash them.
3. Place the mushrooms in a heatproof dish and cover with the remaining ingredients. Mix well.
4. Make sure that the mushrooms are placed next to each other and not on top of each other in the mould.
5. Bake in the oven for 25 minutes. The mushrooms are good once they have softened and most of the liquid has been absorbed.
6. Serve and enjoy.

Nutritional values:
564 kcal | 7 g protein | 9 g fat | 8 g carbohydrates

Minced meat casserole with carrots and potatoes

Preparation time: 45 minutes
Ingredients for 2 servings:
1 tbsp. oil
1 large onion (diced)
100 g carrots (finely diced)
200 g ground beef
20 g corn flour
500 ml beef stock (yeast-free)
400 g potatoes (chopped)
Water for the potatoes
1 tablespoon clarified butter
1 pinch sea salt
1 pinch white pepper
2 tbsp tomato paste

Preparation:

1. Preheat the oven to 200 degrees.
2. Grease the casserole dish with lard.
3. Briefly sauté the onions and carrots in a pan with oil until both have softened.
4. Add the minced meat. Fry for 4-5 minutes.
5. Add the cornflour and stir in.
6. Add the stock. Stir everything until smooth.
7. Add the tomato paste and bring to the boil.
8. Then simmer on a low heat for 15 minutes. Season with salt and pepper.
9. Put the potatoes in a pot with water. Bring to the boil, then cook on low heat for 8-10 minutes.
10. Drain and mash.
11. Add clarified butter and salt. Mix to a uniform mass.
12. Put the mince mixture into the baking dish first, then the potato mixture evenly distributed.
13. Roughen the surface a little with a fork.
14. Bake in the oven for 15-20 minutes.
15. Serve and enjoy.

Nutritional values:

500 kcal | 66 g protein | 62 g fat | 89 g carbohydrates

Mediterranean style chicken and vegetable casserole

Preparation time: 60 minutes + marinating time

Ingredients for 2 servings:

3 tsp olive oil

1 tsp honey

2 tbsp. soy sauce

1 tbsp. chilli sauce

½ jar of cranberries (approx. 100 g)

3 tsp tomato paste

A little salt

1 potato

300 peppers (red and yellow mixed, diced)

100 g courgettes (diced)

1 onion (cut into rings)

1 clove of garlic (crushed)

300 g chicken breast fillet (cut into bite-sized pieces)

2 tomatoes (diced)

1 sprig of rosemary (ready to cook, one part chopped, one part for decoration)

1 thyme sprig (ready to cook, chopped)

1 tbsp chicken stock

Rapeseed oil (quantity as required)

Preparation:

1. Marinate the meat with olive oil, honey, soy sauce, chilli, cranberries, tomato paste and a pinch of salt. Leave to soak for a good hour.
2. In the meantime, preheat the oven to 200 degrees.
3. Sauté the garlic, onion and (chopped) herbs with oil in a pan or pot.
4. Then put everything except the meat into a casserole dish.
5. Salt, pepper and mix well.
6. Put the meat together with the marinade into the casserole dish as a "topping".
7. Pour over chicken stock and garnish with rosemary sprigs (the rest).
8. Cook in the oven for 40 minutes.
9. Serve and enjoy.

Nutritional values:

830 kcal | 88 g protein | 26 g fat | 50 g carbohydrates

Courgette and asparagus chicken casserole

Preparation time: 40 minutes
Ingredients for 2 servings:
400 g green asparagus (washed, ends cut off, lower third peeled)
Water (quantity as required)
A little salt
2 courgettes (stalked)
1 onion (cut into strips)
2 chicken fillets (total: 250 g)
2 tbsp. coconut oil
1 pinch of pepper
100 g crème fraiche (low-fat version with around 15% fat)
1 tsp curry powder
A handful of pine nuts
1 tsp rosemary

Preparation:

1. Pre-cook the asparagus in boiling salted water for 7-10 minutes.
2. Drain and drain.
3. Preheat the oven to 200 degrees.
4. Fry the meat in a pan with coconut fat for 5-6 minutes, turning occasionally. Season with salt and pepper. Remove from the pan and set aside.
5. Sauté the onion in the pan (with the remaining fat there). Add the courgettes and fry briefly. Season with salt and pepper and add curry powder. Remove from the pan and set aside.
6. Dissolve the drippings with the light crème fraiche and bring to the boil briefly. Season with salt and pepper.
7. Arrange the vegetables and asparagus in a baking dish and garnish with the meat on top. Drizzle with the fat cream. Finish with a sprinkling of pine nuts.
8. Cook for 20-25 minutes.
9. Sprinkle the finished casserole with rosemary.
10. Serve and enjoy.

Nutritional values:

820 kcal | 82 g protein | 40 g fat | 24 g carbohydrates

More recipe ideas for neurodermatitis

Other recipes

Quinoa basic preparation

Preparation time: 15 minutes
Ingredients for 4 servings:
150 g quinoa
600 ml water
1 tablespoon olive oil
1 pinch of salt

Preparation:

1. Rinse the quinoa with water.
2. Bring the water to the boil. Cook the quinoa in it (covered) on a low heat for 12-15 minutes.
3. Remove from the heat. Leave to swell for 10 minutes.
4. Salt and refine with olive oil.
5. Serve and enjoy.

Nutritional values:

600 kcal | 12 g protein | 16 g fat | 100 g carbohydrates

Leek-refined apple rolls with marjoram

Preparation time: 30 minutes

Ingredients for 2 servings:

300 g potatoes (floury cooking)
Water for the potatoes (amount as required)
4 marjoram stems (chopped, leaves separately)
The light of a leek (cut into strips)
1 apple (diced)
1 tsp germ oil
1 pinch of salt
1 pinch of pepper
2 slices wholemeal spelt bread

Preparation:

1. Cook potatoes with skin in boiling water for the classic 20-30 minutes.
2. Heat the oil in a pan. Sauté the leeks in it (covered) on a low flame for 5-7 minutes.
3. Add the apple and marjoram. Steam for a good minute. Season with salt and pepper.
4. Drain the potatoes and rinse with cold water. Peel and mash (while still warm) with a potato ricer. Place in a bowl.
5. Add the vegetable mixture to the potatoes. Mix well.
6. Spread the potato and vegetable spread on two loaves of bread. Garnish with marjoram leaves and enjoy.

Nutritional values:

460 kcal | 12 g protein | 4 g fat | 88 g carbohydrates

Mango-Spinach Vegetable Mix with Amaranth

Preparation time: 40 minutes
Ingredients for 4 servings:
700-800 g leaf spinach (prepared ready to cook)
2 bunches spring onions (roughly chopped)
2 mangoes (diced)
2 tablespoons germ oil
1 piece of ginger (around 30 g)
2 tablespoons sunflower seeds
20 g amaranth pops
A pinch of salt
A pinch of cayenne pepper

Preparation:
1. Heat half the oil in a saucepan. Sauté the spring onions over a medium heat (covered) for a good five minutes. Add the spinach. Sauté for another five minutes.
2. Peel and grate the ginger. Also collect the resulting ginger juice and set aside.
3. Add the mango, ginger powder and juice to the pot. Cover and heat on a medium flame for three minutes.
4. Heat the remaining oil in a Teflon pan. Roast the sunflower seeds in it on a low flame for 3-5 minutes.
5. Add the amaranth pops to the pan. Allow to warm through briefly.
6. Salt the mixture in the pot. Place on a plate. Drizzle with the contents of the pan and pepper.
7. Serve and enjoy.

Nutritional values:
960 kcal | 32 g protein | 40 g fat | 110 g carbohydrates

Pasta with courgettes and mushrooms

Preparation time: 40 minutes

Ingredients for 4 servings:

2 courgettes (sliced)
1 aubergine (sliced)
200 g herb mushrooms (cut into thin slices)
20 g Parmesan (finely grated)
1 clove of garlic (crushed)
1 bunch parsley (prepared ready to cook and finely chopped)
4 mint stalks (prepared ready to cook and finely chopped)
400 g shell noodles (or other short pasta)
Water for the pasta
A pinch of salt
2 tbsp rapeseed oil
1 tsp oregano
A pinch of pepper
2 tbsp olive oil

Preparation:

1. Prepare the pasta according to the package instructions.
2. Heat the rapeseed oil in a Teflon pan. Fry the courgettes, aubergines and mushrooms in it over a high heat for 2-3 minutes.
3. Add the garlic, oregano, salt and pepper. Cook on a low flame for 3-5 minutes, stirring constantly. Add the herbs.
4. Drain the pasta. Add 100 ml of the drained pasta water to the vegetables in the pan. Let it boil down a little.
5. Mix the pasta and vegetable mixture together with the olive oil in a bowl.
6. Sprinkle with parmesan, salt and season if necessary.
7. Serve and enjoy.

Nutritional values:

2000 kcal | 80 g protein | 54 g fat | 300 g carbohydrates

Rice porridge with mango

Preparation time: 70 minutes
Ingredients for 4 servings:
180 g brown rice
40 g dried mango
2 tbsp banana chips
500 ml water
450 Milk (low fat)
2 stalks lemon balm (prepared ready to cook)
1 tbsp maple syrup
1 pinch cardamom
1 tsp cinnamon
1 tbsp coconut chips

Preparation:

1. Bring the water to the boil. Add the rice. Bring to the boil again and simmer, covered, on a low flame for 50 minutes until everything is completely absorbed.
2. Chop the dried mango if necessary.
3. Chop the banana chips.
4. Bring the milk and rice to the boil in a saucepan. Then cook for five minutes until creamy, stirring constantly.
5. Add the mango, maple syrup, cinnamon and cardamom to the rice. Simmer for three minutes.
6. Place the rice in bowls and garnish with the remaining ingredients.

Nutritional values:
1100 kcal | 28 g protein | 16 g fat | 196 g carbohydrates

Toast with mango and coconut

Preparation time: 10 minutes
Ingredients for 1 serving:
½ mango (sliced, without peel)
2 slices wholemeal toast
2 tsp margarine
1 tbsp. grated coconut

Preparation:
1. Toast the bread slices. Let cool and spread with lukewarm margarine.
2. Put the mango on the bread.
3. Sprinkle with coconut flakes.
4. Serve and enjoy.

Nutritional values:
344 kcal | 6 g protein | 16 g fat | 43 g carbohydrates

Grits with turkey and yoghurt

Preparation time: 15 minutes
Ingredients for 2 servings:
A pinch of salt
130 g buckwheat groats (medium fine)
2 bunches spring onions (cut into rings)
2 turkey escalopes (cut into strips)
1 tablespoon olive oil
50 g Frankfurt herbs (mix homemade in equal parts borage, chervil, sorrel,
burnet, chives, parsley and cress)
A pinch of pepper
150 g low-fat yoghurt
500 ml water

Preparation:

1. Bring 500 ml of water to the boil. Salt lightly. Sieve and rinse the buckwheat groats. Drain briefly, then add to the water. Bring to the boil again, stirring constantly.
2. Then cover and leave to swell on a low heat for 5-7 minutes. Stir occasionally.
3. Add the spring onions to the grits. Simmer for another five minutes (covered).
4. Fry the turkey breast pieces with oil in a pan for 3-4 minutes on both sides until golden brown.
5. Prepare the Frankfurt herbs ready for cooking. Add 2/3 of them to the grits. Season with salt and pepper.
6. Mix the yoghurt in a bowl until smooth.
7. Put the grits together with the turkey pieces on plates. Sprinkle the rest of the herbs on top. Add the yoghurt and serve.

Nutritional values:
1070 kcal | 92 g protein | 22 g fat | 120 g carbohydrates

Pasta with courgette sauce

Preparation time: 25 minutes

Ingredients for 4 servings:

400 g ribbon noodles (wholemeal)
A little salt
2 courgettes (spiralised or very finely sliced)
2 tbsp olive oil
A little pepper
50 ml vegetable stock
A handful of herbs of your choice
20 g parmesan (grated)
Water for the noodles

Preparation:

1. Prepare the pasta with water (salted) according to the package instructions.
2. Sauté the courgettes in a pan with oil over a medium heat.
3. Pepper, pour in the stock. Leave to infuse for another three minutes.
4. Prepare the herbs - if not already done - ready for cooking.
5. Drain the pasta. Mix with courgettes in a bowl. Add the rest of the ingredients. Mix well.
6. Serve and enjoy.

Nutritional values:

1592 kcal | 64 g protein | 36 g fat | 224 g carbohydrates

Popcorn a la Amaranth

Preparation time: 20 minutes
Ingredients for 1 serving:
3 tbsp. amaranth seeds
Optional: add to muesli

Preparation:
1. Cover the amaranth in a preheated pot without oil.
2. Make sure that the heat is not too high. It is best to use a transparent pot lid. This way you can still react if the grains burn.
3. Finished as soon as the grains have almost completely softened after the exhausts.
4. Serve individually as a snack or as a muesli ingredient and enjoy.

Nutritional values:
282 kcal | 1 g protein | 2 g fat | 12 g carbohydrates

Quick polenta

Preparation time: 25 minutes

Ingredients for 2 servings:

500 ml water

150 g corn semolina

Optional: 1 tsp stevia

Optional: frozen fruit (quantity as required)

Preparation:

1. Bring the water to the boil in the pot.
2. Add the corn semolina, stirring constantly.
3. Leave to swell for a good 15 minutes. Stir occasionally.
4. Add a little frozen fruit and/or stevia (optional).
5. Serve and enjoy.

Nutritional values:

1088 kcal | 7 g protein | 1 g fat | 56 g carbohydrates

Avocado spread with onions

Preparation time: 10 minutes

Ingredients for 2 servings:

150 g avocado

60 g raw onions

A pinch of salt

1 tablespoon lemon juice

Wholemeal bread (for topping)

Preparation:

1. Pick the flesh out of the avocado.
2. Mash the meat with a fork.
3. Sprinkle with lemon juice. Sprinkle with salt.
4. Dice the onions very finely and add to the mixture.
5. Put on bread and enjoy.

Nutritional values:

481 kcal | 2 g protein | 11 g fat | 3 g carbohydrates

Cucumber soup with potatoes

Preparation time: 35 minutes

Ingredients for 4 servings:

5 tbsp olive oil

2 large onions (finely diced)

600 g potatoes (peeled, diced)

800 ml water

A little pepper

1 tsp basil

1 tsp thyme

1 tsp parsley

2 cucumbers (seeded, peeled, diced)

Preparation:

1. Heat the oil in the pot.
2. Sauté the onions in the pot.
3. Add the potato and herbs to the pot. Fill up with water.
4. Cook for a good five minutes.
5. Add the cucumber pieces to the pot. Cook until it is nice and firm to the bite.
6. Scoop out about a quarter of the contents of the pot and set aside.
7. Gently blend the remaining contents of the pot with a hand blender.
8. Pepper the drained vegetables and add them back to the puréed remaining soup.
9. If necessary, dilute the soup with water and serve.

Nutritional values:

3400 kcal | 20 g protein | 31 g fat | 112 g carbohydrates

Chickpeas with rice and chicken from the pot

Preparation time: 35 minutes

Ingredients for 4 servings:

250 g chicken breast fillet (cut into bite-sized pieces)
1 can chickpeas (rinsed, drained)
800 g broccoli (in florets)
250 g rice (wholemeal)
1 tbsp curry paste (mild variety)
400 ml coconut milk (unsweetened)
1 onion (diced)
1 clove of garlic (crushed)
1 pinch of salt
2 tbsp rapeseed oil
300 ml water

Preparation:

1. Cook the rice according to the package instructions.
2. Heat the oil in a pot and brown the meat in it.
3. Then set the meat aside.
4. Now sauté the onion and garlic in the pot until translucent.
5. Add the curry. Sweat briefly.
6. Deglaze with coconut milk and water. Salt.
7. Add the broccoli. Bring to the boil once. Then simmer for five minutes.
8. Add the chickpeas and meat. Mix well and leave to stand for a few minutes.
9. Finally, season to taste if necessary and serve with rice.

Nutritional values:

2480 kcal | 118 g protein | 122 g fat | 243 g carbohydrates